MONIKA HERCEG

CLOSED SEASON

DESIGN & LAYOUT
Nikša Eršek

PUBLISHED BY
Sandorf Passage
South Portland, Maine, United States
IMPRINT OF
Sandorf
Severinska 30, Zagreb, Croatia
sandorfpassage.org

ORIGINALLY PUBLISHED AS
Lovostaj by Jesenski i Turk in 2019.

COVER ART
Danijel Žeželj

PRINTED BY
Znanje, Zagreb

Sandorf Passage books are available to the
trade through Independent Publishers Group:
ipgbook.com / (800) 888-4741.

Library of Congress Control Number: 2025936580

ISBN: 978-9-53351-531-1

This book is published with financial support by
the Republic of Croatia's Ministry of Culture and Media.

MONIKA HERCEG

CLOSED SEASON

translated by MARINA VEVEREC

SAN-
DORF
PAS-
SAGE

SOUTH PORTLAND | MAINE

To my daughter, Kim, and poets

CONTENTS

•

A PROLOGUE FOR GYNOPHOBIA

Falling into the garden, the serpent brings knowledge:
the universe is a vacuum balloon
the apple quantized and nobody gets it
until Newton is struck

Newton, struck by what?
asks Eve with her mouth full, her forked tongue flicking
out
You mean how gravity stretches out the light?
Look! Even my navel is the center
around which the whole planetary system
revolves
as if I'd swallowed the apple whole
And, no, god, you cannot see me naked

But you, Adam, come, cross the river
I'll bear you, Adam,
a 10/10 Apgar algorithm,
DNA, dark matter,
kinetic energy, moon landing
As a little girl I carved eons
but then god's lips spewed out the oceans,
made them boil with other forms of life
now I'm stuck sleeping in the biography of the TV set
my heart ticking in synchronicity with a clock
that doesn't believe in time,
but knows a dinosaur evolves into a bird

Lift up the toilet lid, Adam!

I've shut out the light,
the dirty surface always slackens
under persistent hands

The serpent hisses even sincerer:
I, too, love you, Adam, but you've got to understand
I'm no longer a woman since we'd eaten that fruit
for I now know for certain
where the god's spine broke
and how many solar masses
such a black hole weighs

MARY'S MONOLOGUE TO VENUS OVER A HEAVENLY COFFEE

Out of joy I bite my lip impatiently,
the tilt of the wind in the glass
makes the stillness of water all the more beautiful
Beauty means nothing unless it turns a profit,
the millennia have you shaped into a Barbie
without any vertical thoughts on politics or art
Teeth bared into a proper smile mean nothing,
although a smile is as explosive as a hijacked plane
So much danger hidden behind a hollow laugh!
Nothing, they mean nothing unless the cavities
fit a cataclysm
or at least a calamity, an erased country
or the belly of a gluttonous president
Your foot dipped into the horizon of another planet
means nothing
unless they can fertilize you,
unless they can plant into you
so as to be pulling, always pulling
at your nose, your hair, your cheeks,
the sprouted seedlings out of you

I'm still losing hair even here in heaven,
yet to relieve my postpartum scalp
That's how I've been chronicled for all eternity, as a
deflated ball
from which they had squeezed a god into the country
and film industry
Nobody asks me what it's like to be a spectator
to the documented suffering of my own flesh and blood
All of us in heaven, divine and blind
to the number of stress-induced strokes
or the depressed little hearts
attracted too greatly toward the mass of the dark,
we are a cog in the wheel of some pointless war,
nothing but fuel feeding the fires
in the ovens of concentration camps

And then nothing
All of it, for nothing

Who's got the strength left to explain
that from these ashes
the soul had nowhere else to migrate
but to the first brick
of the tall chimney?

BODY

I gave birth to a son and dreaded his nature,
bore holes in plates,
day after day I overspilled meals with prayers
Converted, bone by bone, loudly
slipped out of some other god's fist
You hear me? My son will never set a cat on fire

Still a cat is merely a structure of agility,
nothing in her paws drives the day
at least not strong enough to make her survive the last
war
Irradiated, she'll grow three heads
and her kittens will glow like light bulbs
Filled with radioactive meaning
she'll be a predator lurking from a distance,
a tenderness that yields a slow death
The neighborhood boys will light cat tails like
firecrackers,
shove the firecrackers in cats' asses, watching as their
guts
outshine the spring explosions of flowers
The blazing cats will jump into our beds
like Molotov cocktails
for the final cuddle

In days to come, closing their eyes to the nature of boys,
all the neighborhood women will burn like the cats

I don't understand why you get so distrustful
You know I bore us a son tough enough
to turn into a girl
when you're not looking

She must've grown up that day
the puss put on the boots,
took away the clarity of her sex
Nothing could be done

PREPARING THE BODY

In the morning we're told to line up and wait
Our turn to have the probe fastened
to our pregnant stomachs
a centipede growing impatient
in the bloodstream of the hospital ward

We listen
The brains of migrant birds calibrate their compasses,
a cyclone engraves March into the backbone of January,
outside the window the bird engines
hum louder than the tiny hearts

Can one live inside a heron and not disrupt its magnetic
sense?

With the thawing wind the brain bark will loosen up,
and tonight I'll dream about
two, three of us
having breakfast, together
Our children resembling the kids in ads,
smiles multiplied by jam

We listen
Our wrists swell with anxieties,
carcinomas slumber
under the unkind nurses' tongues

Through the antiseptic tunnels
the steps of monitor machines and IV stands
clank the loudest
always coming in pairs like procreation
As they're walking through
our bodies grown for the occasion,
we seem to feel
god's hooves
pattering against our skin

HUNT

We've had to wait for our wombs to transform
light into mass, cruelty into birth
then the reforestation of Borneo could begin
I often find you with your face buried into the mournful
stumps
and I know it's your way of asking me
if it even makes sense
forcing anyone to survive the world
in this time and place

Mother said to me:
When the milk sounds with screams
you keep courageously silent like a fallen trunk
She has said the body is porous
so do not care if someday you find
the inside of your heart reflected
in the pattern on the tablecloth
A bad mother carries the genetic modification of
affection
A bad mother sometimes gives birth to a good mother

Other women said to me
Your feet will grow bigger
not from giving birth
but from all the words
Inches away from my belly
they're inspecting my measurements
My dandruff's public dance,
the conifer forest on my upper lip,
how I divide autumn into thirds,
inflating a solid skeleton into my stomach
like a glassworker
creating a stable shape

They watch me stroking my belly
cooing in my mother tongue
to the beeches, wolves, nettles
all secretly
collapsing
into a single being

CLOSED SEASON

After climbing two hundred and twenty stairs
hips come loose like hinges and
a child's hiccup echoes through the pelvis
as if the belly button ate the hypocenter

My downstairs neighbor spent months
collecting drops in plastic basins
in each of the rooms
Who's to know exactly when
the pipe in her bathroom broke

This week they'll drill through her walls
to look for the crack

Temperatures have dropped below zero,
she's freezing with fear
her milk won't flow
These sorts of days, when people stick to their shells like pistachios,
secretly slip into quarter loaves of bread at the checkout counter
and with no one to appeal to

This morning
Frost has lain heavy
over the dead does
even though
it's the closed season

A FIRST-RATE BIRD

Preparing to migrate, they spill commas all around,
the probability of their wombs being empty once again
ripens into certainty

A mother is a solid-boned house sparrow

She blows all proof of Earth's roundness off the horizon,
kernels the world into a seed for a single snack
then folds her chirping down to focus attention
on a favorable forecast
With her head laid on the server's heart
she carefully follows the algorithm
for inflation of clouds

The wind has to inhale up-wing, exhale down-wing

Once a wise bird descended
into an organism suffering from chronic fatigue and asked
why don't I sharply raise my voice at god
Loneliness is insoluble and therefore can cause
traffic jams and heart attacks
I never cook because I'd only be cooking for myself
Loneliness tastes saltless even when I soak in the seawater
for so long that my body grows scales

A realization that wings are as mass-produced as screws
is a sign of a fading trust in the divine
I always suppress memories about my own mechanical
nature
when I plunge back down to my starting point

god often asks me to jump
like a first-rate bird
and overleap his shadow,
the shadow often so huge
my eyes never
leave
the dark

A POEM WITH TWO UNKNOWN VARIABLES

Vera Rubin rhymes the velocities
of rotating galaxies
with raising children properly

As equivalent to:

A poet has a breast that whispers
I'll burst into pieces
When her mouth opens, flocks of purple words
fly out of her stomach,

pills to ease insomnia

MARYAM MIRZAKHANI PUTS THREE SLICES OF INFINITY ON A TOAST WITH CHEESE AND MAYO

I've spent years being a boy, frightened of my thighs,
hiding my body's geographies
under baggy clothes
botany was burgeoning
In your breasts the extinguishing day
swells almost like storm clouds,
yet you, without a second thought, fire up your mind
like a torch
feeding the flames with Riemann surfaces
well aware that summer's heating up the tumors,
that mathematics reveals itself to the persistent
so who cares if the noisy geometries
soon spread to the bones

Before my quantum mechanics class, I still
fearfully resect the woman out of myself
then spend hours on end discussing with Heisenberg
the uncertainty of breasts
which I leave at the doorman's desk

But you, Maryam, your uncovered head
from the obituary in Iranian media
now fiercely stares at the men
offended by your close-cropped hair,
filling their manhood
to every last capillary
with equations of vertical defeat

I LEARNED EMMY NOETHER'S THEOREM IN COLLEGE

I guess it's safe to say, Emmy,
we're two tough pieces of female flesh
It's clear from the lines of our faces
each day was a lonely Wednesday,
symmetrical as the hemispheres of your cleverness

Emmy, Emmy, did mathematics feed you
those seven years when men
took ideas out of your brain
never having paid you on the excuse
there's nothing to you
but numerical values
These days, they would have crammed you into a
computer,
branded you as artificial intelligence
and given you a more seductive name
like Vanda or Irma
then used your algorithm to count
the number of bombs
required on every continent
to avert a nuclear war
I remember the way they peeked under your theorem
in classical mechanics lectures
thinking a mustached man
must be in there somewhere

Emmy, I don't fit into the equation anymore
There are women who believe when it's hunting season
it's fair to push other women
to the brink of extinction
It's then that I feel the sharp symmetry of survival
and know your mother, too,
would stand outside your room
listening
to you crying
but never open the door

DEMETER AFTER A FRUITLESS SEARCH

God opens his eyes
tickling the planet with his eyelashes
the plants abound
Truth be told, the eyelashes are mine,
but I have to lie about my merits
Embryos erupt with screams
but I must not give in when
they, like tumors, settle inside me

Returning from a search, my legs are after all
nothing more than layers of the journey

My daughter, a naive herd of carefreeness
When she's breathing by my side,
concrete resonates with pollen,
galaxies brush past one another
and in these moments of joy, one might easily dream up
spring

My daughter, a devastating yearning
When she's not breathing by my side,
my eyes are buried in graveness
I wear it solemnly and with dignity
deluding myself that everything stops
with my grief:
the fresh air ignores
the presence of the open windows,
people refuse to move,
I delude myself that silence
will keep all lips sealed tight

And in these lonely moments one might easily forget
to bring spring at all

Their faces always cleanly shaven,
smelling of salt and sage,
they have houses
with white façades,
sometimes a daughter,
perhaps one more, then a son
They love them like an extension
of their own spine,
saving for their bedtime,
like Scheherazade,
the sensible part of their tongue
and most often they're warmer than mothers

They start the morning with short black coffee
never revealing their nature
Their bodies a hollow space,
eviscerated,
only a viscous voice
cruising through their cocoons
as they spend their work shift watching
other people's
wounded children
and like gardeners in charge of plants
commanding them
to die die die

THE BEASTS IN ZAGREB PLANTED MY DAUGHTER TO GROW AS A TREE ON MOUNT MEDVEDNICA

They must've mistaken her rose-pink pajamas
for the fur of a careless rabbit
that rolled around in strawberries just seconds before

When the trajectory of death pierced her chest
they must've failed to see
the way her brave yawn rebuked
stunted authorities
then sleepily like a spring flower
returned to the ground

I, A BEAST IN MY APARTMENT, MURDERED MY DAUGHTER JUST MONTHS AFTER GIVING BIRTH

I wrapped her breath in softness
thinking I was helping
the young girl she was to become
because in here her mother
is swallowing down zeros
harder to stomach
than stones

If they wanted to help,
if only they had helped
to split the zeros in two
instead, they said:
Look how happy you are
You have to be happy
What does it matter if you
no longer feel at home
in yourself

A SECOND-RATE FATHER

London fog is a concept I know nothing about
although I always thought that I'd be traveling,
absorbing the world with my hairs, waxing it,
watching as forests, New York, Brač, Niagara Falls
swirl down the drain,
that I'd be dissecting freeways
with the self-confidence of an election campaign,
folding them to fit into the stiff tube of my birth canal

But these days I feel like a fog with a stern
British accent
and I weigh as much as the whole of Earth I never got to
know intimately
The plants are afraid to blossom when I'm near,
because I'd infect their charm forever,
the trees are afraid to spit buds out of their tips
for fear I'd eat their offspring

For months now I've been dancing on the razor's edge of
Sundays
though I'm supposed to be devoting them to family
The truth is, I am lonely,
in waiting rooms, I wish to foster
any old man of refined manners

Poor Persephone, nothing helps,
not even comforting myself with the make-believe
pomegranate seeds
that I playfully press into my belly button
as if they were a tiny Pluto, nobody's place in vacuum
You know, sometimes I dream about us walking in the park,
you're holding my hand like a good-enough father
You're so gentle in my dreams

For six months, Zeus,
for six months you let them
take my clothes off and rape me
in the weightless dark

LISBETH SALANDER MUSES ABOUT FIRE

Father is the most skilled of all mousers
As soon as he turns up
the wrist of my mother snaps
shut by his mousetrap

My child, my pot of overcooked little bones
My wife, my forever chipped glass

He'd open the blinds, this most skilled mouser of ours,
trying to convince us that the pane of glass
won't let photons through if that's what he commands
He's the god of all surfaces
In the dark we wait for the pipeline to announce
the final figures on our gas bill
for the brew of morning to start a pot of coffee,
for the garbage truck to come by
so the voices will dispel the pesky fleas

A fist to the face is always tangent to breakfast

Like a salmon I swim with the day's one-way flow
Escape is not impossible,
but I cannot walk yet

My mind is still trapped in a child's sense of time
but as soon as the clock hands align
I'll gouge out my father's feline eyes
and walk off with them
like a hedgehog
walks off
with apples

LISE MEITNER SPLITS URANIUM, ATOMIC BOMB BITES THE OCEAN

Your father's shadow poured with sentences of encouragement
even when that same shadow outdistanced him
as you rode your bicycles
His arms were always kept open in a wide embrace
so you could keep your equations warm
and, clearing the testosterone-ridden path for you, he'd say:
Autumn is the skull of the Earth airing out,
you have only to look at how these coats wriggle, stuffed with people
But then he

outgrew rooftops and swallowed the first gunshots,
the core of the Earth browning faster than a peeled apple
The world has turned rotten many more times, Lise
My father, for one, drew freeways
on the cats and our legs with birch twigs
We kept running away until
he tore the throat of death open
like that of a pig on a misty morning
then healed it all up into rust red

On a train you transmit your roots to someone else's rich soil
learning the apocalypse, too, is a girl
So you closely listen to the ticking of her atoms
which are no more than a void
obeying statistics

But the little girl is cleaving atomic nuclei apart
when her lights are out
she splits the ribs of the sun's reactions open
little realizing that physics is raising
a spoiled and lazy state,
ever more whimsical with overpopulating of its fur
Purring, rubbing the belly
of the hydrogen bomb,
waiting

A SHORT BREAK FOR A WALK IN THE BACKYARD

Rolling down the meadow comes
the hairless head of Tsvetaeva
and such an asymmetrical aleph
cuts the sentences loose
at once
the key words to
a wireless spring
scatter in the air
Poet:
an unconscious
organ of a poem

THE FLIES

I've stopped trusting the cats
since they won't come near me when I put the food out,
stalling their own taming
making me sit for hours
breathing in the freshly mown sun,
the sawdust of a cut-off nipple
My skin is sloughing off, out of lack of touch
Summer makes it harder to fight my watermelon nature
cut into thin slices
I let the long days dig their teeth into me
and spit out my seeds

I'm waving off the flies gathered round the pieces of my
flesh
as if saying to the furry animals *shoo*
The buzzing drills through the earwax
and I feel the desire for decay
starting to outweigh the desire for friendship
My feet shiver with loneliness
and in the morning, they ache as if
from hours spent standing in the wind

If a cat stays for too long in one place,
her paws sprout and she becomes a tree

Mammography murmurs:
Who is a woman without a breast?

THE ANTIBODY

This borrowed body is
a skyscraper surprised by the persistence of doves,
off its façade flakes the brushing of neighbors,
in the heart of the elevator
the bill collector had a sudden sympathy attack

We've given up defining love as a newborn,
aware we could easily be fooled by a cactus of similar
shape
Our mothers, all excelling in motherhood,
said the emptiness had to do
with my perception of reality
as the volume of a poem
Said it certainly had nothing to do with you

I've been diagnosed with an abyss
In the park I sit calling out to imaginary girls

They already talk like grown-ups
and when they ask Mommy why have you been crying,
I tell them
indifference is
the first degree of dying,
and we are alive, so alive
What I don't tell them is that I've already forgotten
how old they are,
all about their childhood crushes
I don't tell them that in your presence
I never dare to utter
their unborn names

THE CATS

Trust is broken
boys lie to girls they will love them forever
if they pull up their shirts just once and bare the plump
of their bodies
You tell them: My tissue is as limber as an octopus,
in my chest hermaphrodite sea urchins lie dormant
Prick, prick, that's how uniquely I've been defined
A woman is a straight line, an infinity passing through
two points

Nobody talks about what consequence comes with your
petals opening out
Nobody talks about women who spend their entire
pregnancies
vomiting up planets until their knees give out
Nobody talks about soft tissue bruising
too deep to mend

When they took out our next-door neighbor's body, we
witnessed:
Scent cells fled her dead skin,
flocks of men's touches slinked out her flabby thighs,
all of a sudden left hollow like the metal belly of a train
The echoes slammed our faces as we sang of the first
blossom

On that day the sun poured down heavily as if about to
explode
I stepped out of the funeral home into womanhood
reading recipes of arrogant housewives

In the sign language
of women nearing their expiration date
they warn me from a safe distance away:
Stay quiet and come no closer,
jealous cats lurk in the backyards

IN 1940, NADA SREMEC WRITES THAT VILLAGE WOMEN DIE FROM ABORTION AS UNCONTROLLABLY AS IN AFRICA

Their dowry is the drafty air of a birdcage and a long, long needle, which,
whispers the old woman with a wink, is not for darning
Once the redness quakes their foreheads
to the point the seismograph breaks down,
transfigured into wraiths
they try to raise their voices in the throats of neighbors
begging to go and get the doctor
Slapped, the cheekbones plunge into flesh
If others can do it, so can you

They've lost count, at least once every July or August
they spill the jarfuls of unwholesome beetroots
Trampled under men's hooves, herds of unbridled boots
groomed like tigers' stripes, with the same strangling bite

They often walk out to the garden and never return

Schoolgirls without mothers blow on primroses
so ably it hollows out their memory,
then they pickle the nagging winter sniffles,
making the tanks and shells shiver
naked like plane trees

After the imposed amnesia
in some places the fit and unfit mothers resurrect
out of kitchen sinks and stoves,
a helpless colony of moles
in broad daylight
Shrapnel-stocked throats

ANA MAGAŠ MOVES TO A DISTANT STAR AFTER KILLING HER ABUSIVE HUSBAND IN SELF-DEFENSE

The judge says:
We've gathered here in autumn, the time of irreversible fall
You danced with a man
from another planet
The corners of his eyes wrinkled by his native land
devoid of oxygen
What was your husband to say
catching sight of such a disobedient act?

Ana says:
I am here to show my scars,
have you got a telescope to glance
at the marks from fists that turned my limber body stiff?
The knife is but a consequence

The judge says:
Irrelevant, madam.
You, impossible like a cold fusion,
danced, I repeat, with a stranger
Do you actually think you haven't provoked your house to
crack?

Ana leaves unsaid:
The house I live in is a spiral of calcified bruises,
a dead young lady lodges
in my elbow bone healed wrong,
she also rents a place
in my twice-broken ribs
My skull is occupied by the endless court hearings
Soaked as I am from sharing a bed with sprains,
let them take me to rectangular rooms,
rectangular beds
to warm, high-calorie lunches,
walks in rectangular amplitudes
so that my eyes see beyond the perimeters of fear,
so that my newly gained freedom cancels out
the white noise of someone else's tragedies

AILEEN WUORNOS RECONSTRUCTS THE BREAKING OF THE SOUND BARRIER WITH GUNSHOTS

Under the stolen car the world will gather around
a single truth,
and then I'll cheer the bullet I spat out at your lungs
For years, bodies have been sinking into the road
Honesty is laid with asphalt, but I know where the grass
can break through

Now that a new meal has grown out of my thigh
and has been neatly served,
a child who never knew I was his mother will say he's
not hungry
He nibbles the limbs of a gentle surrogate
If the roast tastes too salty, grandfather's liver screams
out imperatives
into my scrunched eyes and strips me down to my bare
sucrose skin of a child
Then the beating
Then dinner

Brother says the seasoned spiders are afoot
their hairy legs cleaning out the specks of darkness
under the bed
All I have to say is I've no memory,
no brother, no name
Then I die
Then breakfast
Two bullets, six, nine
If the omelet of the morning light gets cold,
the child who's been eating out of me will head off to
infinity,
then divide itself by ten and leave again

A threat is sticking out of the asphalt like a daisy tucked
behind the ear
If you touch me,
you'll wake the gun
sleeping under my tongue

MEDUSA BRAIDS HER SNAKES TO BOOST HER SELF-CONFIDENCE

A snake passes the word to the second snake,
to the third snake, to the next:
We see how the day cracks open like a walnut
when your head bangs against the wall,
still, you won't find any compassion inside
You're not the only one we don't understand,
the fan pushes the anguish of July into the face,
but cannot translate summer
It's true, your beauty has been melted down to a snake's length,
and the value of meter is beyond your grasp
What a rattling misanthropy a hair wash has hatched,
who'd have guessed a shampoo could untangle such thoughts

But what's the use of those infrared sensors of yours
or turning skin into stone?
We see you've gulped down a whole herd of sheep,
their wool bleats out a wondrous warmth,
yet your fingers are cold
as if they sense time and again:
in the temple, silence dented windows
and uncoiled under god's tongue
a resolve to shatter you
Your god is a rapist, nonetheless a god,
and he shifts his sin onto your tongue
Were your ankles too loud?
Your knees uncovered?
Did you drop your eyes too rashly to the floor?
Were you too slow to do so?

The metamorphosis of the hairs into snakes
is similar to the question of free will
coming out of the determinists' mouths,
something like boarding a train without a ticket
ready to bend your spine and make a run
but the conductor grabs your arm
something like settling in a plant
to learn how to keep silent,
but it blooms before you even start

EUROPE NEVER SPEAKS OF THE VIOLENCE SUFFERED

After the razor wire, a poem
is easily resurrected
in someone's sleepless night
But don't you go around telling others
about your fear of illiterate men
As they come closer with their butcher hands,
don't you get carried away, like some silly little girl,
by happy endings

You'll meet god
in the guise of a bull,
just like the woman after whom the continent you
migrated to was named,
grasping for humor
under the enduring surface
of your empty stomach

And you won't cry
because this is a world of business,
your heat
that sets into motion
the wheels that brought you
into the wasteland
of a foreign tongue

Europe, stretched to the point of proximity collapse
Europe, the poem should end with a wound,
with a boy floating,
kept above the sea surface
by a war lighter than the salty water,
by a war on the other side of the world,
where we never would've had children
always being watched
by a sniper god
a hand-grenade god

HERA'S ROOM

When his fingers
break out of the traffic gridlock
and stray into the freshly sprouting hairs,
the road promises to lend speed to
my elaborate plan of escape
always devised as a two-step:
Get the window open
jump into a neoprene woman

Out of the tiny hand bones touches splash
faster than anyone gets to shut their eyes
In fact, I can't claim that anyone but me
has their eyes shut
Nobody can save them
Nobody shifts from one woman to another
Nobody, bitter words in a spoonful of chicken soup
Nobody, such a rude nobody
Nobody, called husband on paper,
but who could know for sure?
As soon as he slips out of me like the dark out of a
smoke-fogged room,
underneath my skin
weeping peacocks and god's girls
fall asleep

My silence goes as far as sentences reach
thoughts drifting to the untamable cats
Sometimes I spend hours watching crossroads
to see the cat's soul evaporate
and come back to life for the fifth or eighth time
having encountered velocity firsthand

I say cat, but I mean poetry,
I mean a word hammered to the forehead,
I bleed and I mean an intact book
the smell of which reminds me
of everything I don't have

THE SOUL OF JYOTI SINGH SIPS COFFEE NEXT TO ME, WARNING ME AN IRON ROD COULD SPRING FROM A BYSTANDER

And thrust into you, same as it thrust into me
No, actually it was penetrating,
battering my organs, ferocious
Having survived felt surreal,
to stare up at the coin-shaped sun,
yet feel my consciousness vanish to vapor
You have a daughter; you have software to store yourself
on the present's unshaven face,
I say unshaven because I felt the tickle of hairs
as I tried to tame the onslaught of death

I have a poem for you:

Baked-in capitalism spouts out men's all-tearing jaws
an entire ecosystem has already grown around these
loving fathers,
husbands, grandfathers, brothers,
friends, neighbors, teachers
Beneath the sweet-natured plurality looms a danger
faster than sound
These jaws that
cut and chop
the stringy female nature
enticed by their reflexive courtesy

Sundown, armed with fuss,
I, enraptured with the movie's salty charm,
step aboard the bus naive as daylight
Soon enough the situation gets more painful than
suffocation
They skewer my trust on headlights and slowly
tear the habitat out from my body

They drop me naked by the side of the road
for the weight of midnight to press down on me
and once more impregnate me
with a wet morning,
a seed of infirmity
sown in my every bruise

A SHORT BREAK FOR RESURRECTION

The dusty soul of Sylvia Plath
double-parks
in god's neighborhood
having made up her mind:
in his spite
all day long I'll hunt
his beloved birds of any kind
and grind their hearts into coffee
to talk idly
about his
incurable
fear
of Eve

QUANTUM CINDERELLA

Marble floors draw ovaries into their orbit,
the frost of silence creeps up the barefoot girl's warmth
With no panties on she comes to know
that skin abandons every woman
while washing her husband's back
or while being penetrated by a four-carat crown
The birds leave her heart taking to air on autopilot
and for the umpteenth time
she thinks about her sisters
as a warmth she'll never overcome
certain she is missing them
like everyone misses
taking a beating that could've been predicted after all
In bed, the day is tense
to exhaustion,
furniture sighs in laziness
It's tedious, if not dangerous,
when the prince's arrival
cools the oxygen until it condenses
and drowns her in his embrace

The loud discussions of crows
sweeten her time
When she hears them, she imagines girlfriends
and spends hours talking to them about love in
metaphors
Says love is slaughtered poultry
or a bullet-stricken wing
Many interpretations are possible

Her continent is squashed into a body left untold
Fears are rooms trodden
by women encased in faulty bullets,
women-clouds for the skyline's private collection

And all of it would've been enough
could the sky have been built
under the house

IN ONE OF THE MANY POSSIBLE REALITIES,THE PRINCESS HAS EVOLVED INTO A VICTIM OF DOMESTIC VIOLENCE

The future came too fast,
the future came all too sudden
like a glimpse into one's own shallow happiness
Whatever our thoughts on the charred ground,
it seemed to you that warmth meant more than freedom
The severed fingers of your sisters,
a new forest growing from
your departure, a foster family
But it, too, handed you back over
into his clutches
left stumps on your skin
so you'd stumble
if you ever wished
to say no

If you're smothered by his love,
he restarts your heart on time
Implants your chest, dead or alive,
with electric pulses
all the while cooing to you tenderly:
You're too beautiful
for me to slash
slash
slash

In bed, the digital revolution
is already unfolding
none of it, of course, concerns the loud herd
you care for daily
With your feet
dipped into the neck of the river
you wonder
how come it seems appropriate
to lie down forever
in the water's mouth

MARY JANE KELLY AND ANA (17, OSIJEK, STABBED AND LEFT TO BLEED TO DEATH) CONTEMPLATE THE BLADE

I could be a long-legged antelope
and overleap the city's bloodstream,
if I spent long enough inventing myself I'd probably
ditch the routine of jamming my shoulder against the
week

A knife is as self-assertive
as a black hole at the center of the Milky Way,
but the hand could tremble
It could change its mind
if it figures out this morning,
an unnamed tearfulness condensed
in the bedroom-wall Virgin Mary

Or none of the above

I believe god's hiccups
sometimes set tectonic plates in motion
but I don't believe in a god
fretting over the ants

In much the same way the street is already sprinkled by
his steps,
I sense the carving of my crust will be an artistic act
In any case, life found home in me
as accidently as a river settles the basements
I am a redhead, I am a brunette, just name it,
an inviting space for the afternoon to be spent

He'll retailor my body with a knife
then fall back into a dream
of mother replanting domestic bliss
from one pot to another
the plant yelling out to her
it takes more,
more than water

A WOMEN'S SHELTER

We, the deaf and underfed does
fed on poetry
our fawns
gnawing at our feeble breasts

All of us,
with one foot in
the steel snare
on some meadow miles away

wait for someone to tell us all about
what it's like to have

a safe night

VIŠNJA LJUBIČIĆ'S 2016 REPORT FOUND THAT SOME THREE HUNDRED CROATIAN WOMEN WERE MURDERED IN THE PAST DECADE

And then the crime news
and from the TV screen flows
a report
a pregnant woman was killed,
in front of her ten-year-old son,
by a war veteran
Up until now a quiet and reserved man,
easily mistaken for a barefoot saint,
nay, Jesus himself,
who surely would've helped
had the crucifix above the bed
not been broken in half

Women
paired in electric circuits
Switched on
Switched off
They catch the first tram
then stretch their bruises wearily
hoping the next stop will lead them
to believe they've resurrected
as pure-blooded Marys
whose coming bathes the Earth's belly
in steaming light

Sometimes they leave for work
and never return

Trying to wake them up
schoolboys without mothers
tweak their drunken fathers' noses
which grew bigger with every story they told
of their mothers whoring around
and over the years breached
all the windows and walls,
their snores roaring like combines
before the last harvest

THE POET'S EMANCIPATION

He said: You'll hardly ever break the resistance of
allegory
He, who came out of the womb already a poet,
the placenta feeding him rhymes and rhythm
Me, a country bumpkin,
with an armful of corn ears
that I claim to be words
He said: Poems are no place for a woman
drop that book
you look ridiculous

Then a mattock, the weapon of the crime,
though not, to be clear,
an admission of guilt
Now he soaks the pages
Verbs spike through a lifeless language,
spread like viruses
Strike the birds
What to do with these victims?

It's simple, the poet revealed
before drawing his last breath:
You dress their wounds to make them tame,
and once released
they'll infect the flocks with poetry,
the flocks will pass it on to the antennae, balconies, and
cats,
cats to their owners,
owners to their kids
and on and on

ON THE FIRST ENCOUNTER OF THE POET AND THE POEM

I laid out all the tools to overturn my childhood
and just as I was about to get down to bitter work,
I, a little girl, a lying kernel,
I, a mother, a faulty fruit tree,
split into two, turned compost
for the winged words grown to brush off
the first clouds covering the heart
I could've patiently set
the table with a plate of lies, got ahead of the poem
and drawn its eyes with my finger
so she'd get to see Sundays or a precise reader
I could've applied some makeup on her vowels,
convinced her to make home
under the feathery wings of southern chirruping,
to reverse the book's magnetic poles
I could have, but I instinctively admitted:
In my galaxy, stars are born like ABCs,
the nebulae fizzing with sound changes
My husband a protosun warming my deep faults
petrified like the first fossils
the biggest one: I don't know how
to talk to people

That's how the poem marked me in her calendar,
as an extraordinary event:
You are a little girl whose physics cannot be spelled out
You are a woman whose output of happiness
is at odds with your tuber origin

Turn your syntax my way, like I'm painting your portrait,
says the poem, and her words reach for my hair like a daughter's
Rearranging strands of hair and our encounters,
moving our embraces around like living-room furniture

What can poetry rouse to life
except the swelling sadness,
a woman endlessly far from the land,
an empty parliament, ransacked villages,
a loud silence of extinction,
which pooled yesterday
in the kid's breakfast

THAT POEM, THERE'S NO WAY THAT WAS ME

In my head, your fingers on my skin again
to reconstruct a sentence,
an electricity that cannot
wash me clear of the darkness

In my limbs, mirrored gestures,
my mother's door-slamming habit
that imminently tainted summer with cruelty
Years later they'll be saying
I'm abnormally rigid,
that this absence of tender care
would infect whomever I tried to love

I stood there with hands cupped over my ears
when love blew up in my face

I'll focus my thoughts on the lunch I burned,
on whether you'll catch a cold walking out
with only a short-sleeved checked shirt on
I'll pretend
I happened to sneeze just now, the exact moment
when you've reclaimed
a cubic meter of air,
unbothered by eggs broken
under my heartbeats
But it's not love that brings you to your death,
it's the unpaid bills
the unblemished caterpillars
in my belly are telling me,
aware they've been denied
the possibility of a butterfly

That's no way to talk to your heart
It knows nothing
about the average income
of an underpaid schoolteacher
or of a poet who takes herself too seriously
Learn from your heart
about showing respect for the dark
Only when making love
do not turn the lights out

ANOTHER POEM WITH TWO UNKNOWN VARIABLES

At first the women have been vaporized
into laboratory mice
and bookworms
through men's hands,
but then
Jefimija
recklessly
like Eve
took a bite
of a poem,
Marie
of a vial

As equivalent to:

I want to die of poetry
or knowledge
Let it be radioactive
handed down to daughters
by word of mouth
like the wound
of the first fall

NOT THE POET, BUT MARIA GOEPPERT MAYER COULD'VE UNDISTRACTEDLY DREAMED ABOUT ATOMIC NUCLEI

You could've sprouted your shoots from a crater on Venus
and overgrown the young lined up at the employment
office
with your enthusiasm to work for the equations
Your love for physics
had a nuclear reactor
which made it easy for you to melt through men's distrust,
volunteer, volunteer, volunteer

For they refused to believe
in your solutions even when
the universe said out loud:
Hello, Maria, Cosmos speaking,
I'll move into your floral dresses
to explain myself
through proton hearts
Just listen!

I imagine your theorems growing
out of the desk in your stuffy office
and maybe I am jealous
because you could dive headfirst
to the bottom of mathematics
without a concern about whether there's anything to eat
No really, what is there to eat for dinner
amid these crops of numbers?

I can't seem to forget the little girl in a cornfield
picking stars instead of kernels
The boredom of a life with no one to talk to
that led her sometimes to a black hole
which would spit her right out
the same way education
spits out penniless young girls
As it turns out, I was only a lucky one

And maybe I am a bit jealous, Maria,
because you stubbornly held on to your dreams
even when hate made it rain shrapnel,
because you always believed
in reality's microscopic heart
and that in the possibility of such a world
lies the cure for all mankind

ADA LOVELACE IS CONSUMED BY COMPUTING LOGIC, LATER TURING IS CONSUMED BY ADA

The London rats gladly
leap into cats' open mouths,
to translate: the city is so starved
zero meanders through the streets
The same zero you feel
in your strict upbringing,
and when no one is looking
you cut out love
as soon as it oxidizes
under your skirt
From where you stand,
the force of math drives reality
even your husband's

Who never objects, and when you drift off to dream
he covers you with a blanket and lets
the giant machine absorb you from π
to infinity
while in the same dream there's Erato,
surrounded by cats, demented,
cleaning couches and cursing at your father

Down on the street the stench as if the night were washed
in urine,
the creaking of women whose corsets are growing too tight
and once the numbers finally tire you out
you settle down in your father's poem, Childe Harold,
so the acid in the soil can eat through both of you, together,
though you've never met

except in chromosomes
which have been rewired
not to speak in verses
but in binary code
to Alan Turing's
neurons

JOCELYN BELL'S TELESCOPES BRING THE VOID CLOSER TO THE POET

In the navel of the big bang
they were teaching you to sew buttons on shirts,
that the universe lies inside a pot
that the freshly picked cauliflower heads
are the only bursting stars

They never told you a woman could
break open the night like an egg if she wanted to,
that she could point a telescope out of her bra
somewhere
other than at the faces of women, looking to find
sprouts of mustache
that must be cut as short as talk
Louder, you must be louder
when translating the dead cores of warmth

It's the worst when your eyes burn with spring's
rotation,
the pulsar tilts vacuum into a point
You collect all that scatters into your antenna,
optics swell with irregular signals

You say you've forgiven them
for how they laughed you off then kept the sky all for
themselves
What did they know, Jocelyn, about your telescopes,
which you could've brought to maturity in your spinal
cord
easily like milk to cheese

Now that you're hunkered down in catalogues of the sky
you fail to notice that happiness
changes the properties of the poets' bodies, too,
reluctantly as salt restructures the icy roads
They put on ambition over the dark circles under their
eyes
but then life floods them
busy with the kids, cats, iron, kitchen
they forget to breathe
It's that simple, Jocelyn

THE TRAINS, OR ON THE POET'S LOVE FOR VRONSKY

In the train's rapid motion
punctuation and shapes of animals near the tracks
dilute with haze
A landscape nonsensically defined as a metaphor,
growing a torso of a forest or farming poems along the railroad,
god's coughs in the electrical grid

Falling silent is an attempt at simultaneity of all possible outcomes
such is the way a journey breaks the bodies to fragments
In the most likely reality
a broken-up sentence just now brought a galaxy to light
and I am that one suicidal fly in a swarm,
shouting above the uproar of quarreling tracks

I should've known that orderliness, not love,
was the proper way to communicate with the world
The neatly arranged bones, the four seasons,
the metamorphoses,
the poems listed in alphabetical order, an herbarium
This something between us wreaked havoc in the grainfields,
now we are hunger and privation,
displaced from our hearts to these battered seats

Before the universe closes its eyes again
tell me, Vronsky,
are your fingers still inside my flesh?

A TOUGHER MADAME BOVARY, OR ON THE COMMONPLACE OF THE POET

It's always like this when we don't understand each other,
the body shrivels to singularity,
the casing too small to hold in all the unease

A tougher woman hatches inside the weaker one like a tortoise
on days when rain outwits the little girls inside them
After I've uttered
traffic accidents
I spend the morning recycling the trajectories of crabs
that escaped the net
like the structure of Emma slipped past the men

Come on, you know what icy sidewalks are like,
your foot slips against all the sleep lost
and then letters rip through your skin
Just when you were about to grapple with the concept of women's poetry,
digest the metaphor thoroughly like a pork chop,
and say vegetarianism is a much-needed retreat,
a cleansing ritual

Come on, you know what it's like, a poem has strong roots,
why pretend you could write something important

Like:

My husband will break apart into other husbands
and once I put him back together
all I'll find is the bottom
of unvoiced negations

POET IN THE SUMMER

The inevitability of the day rolls
down the sweaty back into a poem
like a stroller
loaded with Venus's sulfur and sadness
But perhaps the sky could rip open someday
when the navel of the evening sneezes
into our dinner
pouring out hordes of aliens
stinking of rotten eggs
And god,
someone's fiery, resigned god
who merely takes down anecdotes
of how our mascara strokes
sweep away the clumps of guilt
of beating our kids,
of beating our dogs,
of smothering newborn kittens,
to the tips of our eyelashes

We're soon doomed to suffocate in the toxic jar
if someone doesn't come up with a way of cutting off
the chimneys
It's bound to happen on a sultry summer day
resembling the one in which I took my first beating
The flies gulped down chunks of sky louder than the jets

Dogs don't, but children do remember everything
They remember your scornful looks,
remember the exact place
where the whip met the flesh
and cut
Deeper and
deeper
through the layers of clothes

It's the hardest in summer
with nowhere to recoil
but to one's naked self

POET DEFINED

The checkpoint is midnight, I'll write about that time
when a few years back the noun that stripped Cinderella bare
dropped into our soup, I'll write about make-believing a childhood
in a ten-by-ten room, about the cucumbers bought on sale,
the bitter taste in which we bathed
as if it could nourish us with summer

You pass me the sour cream, the chill sucking in the green,
the first cucumbers we've had since the war, but to me it's a faint memory
You tell me that I used to be chatty and insatiable as a child,
that I never said thank you or knew when to stop,
that our hunger for fresh vegetables
shrunk the night and like kittens we rested in its lap

My fears have always been evenly coated with lime,
the abrading, stifled sinking creeks
All the darkness I've kept in my hair was coming loose,
trickling onto my plate;
you didn't know how to comb it off me or squeeze it out,
and for years it has seemed like I was nearing the bottom,
trapped in an endless fall

Lately as I drift off to sleep

the sea we once got to meet
engulfs me
The dolphins on my swimsuit can eat
any menacing eye gazing up from the depths
I'm terrified, knowing
that I'm too far from shore,
that I'm a dot amid the blue,
and I'll never fend off
the vast space

Sometimes before the poem begins I still
find myself adrift in the wet darkness
which might as well be
any bit of midnight
time when hunger is easily tricked,
but I've never given up
trying
to push myself
against nothing at all

POET BANISHED THE BEASTS FROM HER GARDEN

Still yesterday she saw:
in the park, a father telling his five-year-old son
he's crying like a little girl

Yesterday she saw:
in the park, a father pulling the grounded birds by ears

They spend an hour sitting on the swings in fear
and when he's not watching
slyly smiling
they leave with the wind

THE WIDOW'S WEEDS, OR ON THE POET'S EAVESDROPPING ON DEATH

Last night she tossed a water-drenched pupil,
a bone that no longer fits into the socket
after a nightlong friction on the bones of another,
out of her apron and down the sewer,
let out a relieved sigh and passed water
thick with shoals of unborn carp
Maybe someone is sensing
she had far more love
than could fit inside a two-room apartment,
now empty but of insomnia

I resonate as if I were her core
when pressing my ear
against their front door

Her black widow's weeds quivering like vacuum
at the beginning of the universe

THREE POETS FROM AN UPROOTED MAGNOLIA

This time of the year, the morning papers grow under beds
and the poets harvest the letters

The first poet prudently replants language
so she'd lure in the squirrels,
their wondrous tails bristle with state affairs
there must be no talk about, e.g., someone is ripping off
the pension funds,
the system is unsustainable

The second poet opens cans of food with her nails,
inside the peas squirm,
our language is too ancient to treat current affairs
Finances have overgrown the greenery of the city
enclosed in the buds of plastics

The third poet could be as tame as a pet,
but she's aware that poor handling of waste
makes recycling impossible,
even when it comes to the sentence at the heart of a tree

The poets collect disappointments,
entering all people with equal devotion,
without discrimination,
not realizing I have to put on makeup
for work to please
the machines printing out time
This morning, they uprooted
a magnolia in full bloom
to plant dredgers in its place

For a long time, the purple kept vigil over the road,
now the time's come for the words between us
to turn heavy,
like concrete
on which poems
cannot alight

A SHORT BREAK FOR GRIEVING

Picture this, amid a timely death
briefly turning around
to show off her enviable figure in a bikini,
Szymborska sits,
sprinkled with the finely ground sugar of solitude,
and checks out my lungs,
for fear
of carcinogenic poetry

THE WIND, OR ON THE POET'S GOD

The fuses of the universe blew,
it just so happened that something fills nothing at the speed of light

I get that it's a matter of laziness, our exponential growth
is unsustainable
You begin to see you cannot keep your garden in order and then

Instead of cleaning you start piling up souls,
exerting atmospheric pressure
You had good intentions, mothering instincts, yeah, I know

The burdening loneliness,
you hoped at least a fellow woman would understand

For some time now I also know people don't like
having love come nowhere near their tongue

There's no use for such false words
I release them to join the birds, to get them closer to you
to shame you, to make you feel their bite

Sometimes our eyes meet, and weeks cancel out one another,
you enter my body insufferably
and I think I can feel the creation,
irreconcilable differences

It’s been so long since we last spoke

Now you only watch
at night
when I clip my nails
and masturbate

POET ON FRIDAYS

During the night petals fall from the embarrassed body

A cat falls asleep on her belly,
one that meows purified poetry
which won't make squealing noises
when the unrealized poems
slide over the tongue

The misery of people who visit the bank is as contagious
as herpes,
she checks her armpits for paralyzing lumps,
although she always makes sure to wipe clean the
counter
on which they rest their state-stained elbows
while pestering her with nervous questions
can anything be done
to get them out of the red

She wonders,
when asked what she does for a living,
whether she should say
a bank teller
or a poet that runs on internal combustion
Poems are amassing stress in a caterpillar
then the wait
Much like loans, after all,
you take out something from the depth,
which you never talk about with friends,
then pay back greater sums
to a more balanced self you hope to become
In the end it's all a matter of time:
a mole expelling winter out of her blindness
a plant impatiently awaiting pollen

Repeating that mantra offers more comfort
than spring's immediate return,
a one-time love, newly bought shoes
In truth, it offers more comfort
than the training wheels on a bike
or storing fat in your thighs

MARY'S MONOLOGUE TO THE POET OVER AN EARTHLY COFFEE

You've got eyes so you wouldn't think you've got a mouth
for various permutations of bread, meat spread, starvation,
so you'd believe living inside a poem
can be as exciting as living inside a bird

Words can travel at the speed of light,
but besides them, nothing seems to heal
so simultaneously

You're a confident poet
your finger refracts trajectories of comets
the thoughts that words can fill
an empty room or a child's hunger

Behind you women gather to decipher the traces in your
coffee,
will you blossom or burn out,
will you even fit into such predictable grounds
Poetry is, I paraphrase,
the possibility to separate "here" from "being,"
and once you rid yourself of your mundane properties
you can freely radiate into the world
until you dissipate

I was made up
for no one to ever consider my feelings
in the name of a higher purpose
for no one ever to ask whether immaculate conception
is a form of rape,
for there to be talk behind my back, though they know
their tongues will fall off
for them to dare even force happiness upon me

And if you ever find yourself on the brink of such an abyss
demand a divorce
and full custody

ABOUT THE AUTHOR

Born in 1990 in Sisak, Croatia, Monika Herceg is a poet, playwright, essayist, feminist, activist, and editor at Fraktura Publishing; she is the recipient of dozens of literary awards, her poems, books, and plays have been translated into more than twenty languages, and she is the recipient of the City of Petrinja Award in 2024 and the City of Zagreb Award in 2025.

In 2017, she received the Goran Award for Young Poets for her debut manuscript *Početne koordinate* (*Initial Coordinates*). The book was published in 2018 and was awarded the Kvirin Award for Young Poets, the Fran Galović Prize for the best literary work on the topic of homeland and/or identity, the Slavić Award for the best debut published in 2018, and the Macedonian Bridges of Struga International Poetry Award for the best debut.

Lovostaj (*Closed Season*) won the national literary award Prozak for the best unpublished manuscript by an author under 35 in 2018 and was published in 2019. In 2020, her third book of poetry, *Vrijeme prije jezika* (*The Time Before The Tongue*), was published and awarded the Zvonko Milković Award for the best collection of intimate and/or native themes.

She was awarded the biennial Polish prize European Poet of Freedom 2024 for *Lovostaj* and the Central European Award for Young Writers 2024.

She has also won several regional prizes for short stories, including the Ranko Marinković Award, the Biber regional award for short stories on reconciliation (twice), and the Lapis Histriae regional award.

She received the award for the best drama of the Croatian National Theater in Zagreb for her play *Gdje se kupuju nježnosti* (*Where to Buy Tenderness*), which premiered in 2021. She has won several awards for drama scripts, including the most prestigious Marin Držić Award twice, as well as the award of the Croatian National Theater in Mostar twice. Her plays are broadcast as radio dramas on Croatian Radio. *Zakopana čuda* (*Buried Miracles*) was also filmed as an experimental film.

In 2022, a collection of her plays, *Ubij se, tata* (*Kill Yourself, Dad*), was published. She has also written and directed several radio plays for Croatian Radio and Television. Her play *Beautiful Interiors: Zagreb* premiered in May 2025 at Arterarij in Zagreb.

She received the Fierce Women Award in 2021 for her activist work.

Currently, she is working on a novel, and she is also developing her first screenplay for a feature film, having won the Zora Dirnbach and Bruno Bauer projects for script development. Additionally, she is finishing her first documentary short movie, in which she is both screenwriter and director.

She is a member of the editorial board of the magazine *Poezija* of the Croatian Writers' Association and the manager of various cultural programs at the Croatian Writers' Association and PEN Centre, where she also serves as a member of the Management Board. She is also a part of Versopolis, a European platform for poetry.

Herceg is the curator of Caffe Europa, part of the Dilemma project led by the Polish Borderland Foundation, which brings different voices from Central Europe into dialogue. She writes a monthly cultural column for one of the leading Croatian magazines, *Telegram*.

ABOUT SANDORF PASSAGE

Sandorf Passage publishes work that creates a prismatic perspective on what it means to live in a globalized world. It is a home to writing inspired by both conflict zones and the dangers of complacency. All Sandorf Passage titles share in common how the biggest and most important ideas are best explored in the most personal and intimate of spaces.